GET ALIGNED!
10 PRINCIPLES
to Grow Your Internal Brand

Jerome Joseph
CSP, Global Speaking Fellow, PMC

© Jerome Joseph
2nd Edition 2018

All content included is the property of Jerome Joseph and is protected by Singapore copyright laws.

Purchase of this document gives you the exclusive right to access the document for personal use only.

No part of the document may be reproduced, duplicated, copied, disseminated, circulated, sold, exploited for any commercial purpose, stored in a retrieval system or transmitted by any means including but not limited to electronic, mechanical, digital and manual means without the written permission of the publisher. Any unauthorized use terminates the permission granted by Jerome Joseph.

Jerome Joseph does not have any rights of any nature whatsoever in the trade marks, logos or any interest in any third-party companies and their products.

Table of Contents

About the Author 5

Introduction & Purpose 6

The Story of Internal Branding 7

Principle 1: Give your Employees a Cause not a Job 9

Principle 2: Listen to your Employees 12

Principle 3: Lead your Employees to the Level of
Passionate Commitment 15

Principle 4: Create Brand Champions 18

Principle 5: Deliver a Consistent Brand Message to your Employees 21

Principle 6: Create Alignment between a Compelling Employee
Promise and Delivery 24

Principle 7: Ensure your Employees Deliver a Branded
Customer Experience 27

Principle 8: Build Brand Leaders 30

Principle 9: Ensure that you Recruit On-Brand Employees 33

Principle 10: Recognise and Reward 36

Bonus Principle: Symbols, Stories & Rituals 39

Conclusion 42

Our Internal Brand Framework 45

Our Keynotes and Workshops 46

Talk To Us 47

Let's Get Started

ABOUT THE AUTHOR

Jerome Joseph
CSP, Global Speaking Fellow, PMC
Chief Experience Officer

Jerome Joseph CSP, Global Speaking Fellow, PMC is an award-winning Brand & Customer Experience Strategist & Speaker focused on Brand Strategy, Brand Experience, Internal Branding, Personal Branding and Customer Experience.

He is a bestselling Author of 7 books on Branding. He has over 22 years of experience, worked with over 1000 brands, including many Fortune 500 companies, in 33 countries. The combination of real life consulting experience with Fortune 500 companies, global expertise and proven speaking skills makes Jerome a sought-after speaker in the market. With his highly infectious personality, fast-paced and interactive style of speaking and storytelling, audiences can expect to be entertained while attaining a wealth of great insights.

His keynotes and workshops are simply not to be missed! Jerome runs programs and keynotes ranging from Internal Branding (Building Brand Champions in your organisation), Brand Mastery (Strategies to Build a World Class Brand), Branded Customer Experience, Personal Branding and Asian Brand Strategies based on Lessons from the top 30 Asian Brands.

Awards

Jerome holds the Certified Speaking Professional (CSP) designation which is held by the top 12% speakers in the world as an award for speaking expertise. He was awarded the prestigious Global Speaking Fellow in 2015 as the 2nd Singaporean to earn this award and the 30th speaker in the world to achieve this. Currently less than 1% of speakers globally hold this designation. He also holds the Practising Management Consultant (PMC) designation awarded to experienced industry veterans in consulting. Jerome was recognised as a Top 30 Global Brand Guru in 2018 and is the only Asian based in Asia to make the list.

Jerome Joseph is the author of best-selling book "Internal Branding: Growing your Brand from Within"

INTRODUCTION & PURPOSE

Introduction

If employees know why their brand matters, they are more likely to strive to perform their jobs better. Brands that want to be successful must tap into the full potential of their employees where they can activate their employees as powerful agents of change for their brand.

They need their employees to be ready to embrace their brand and put it to action. They need employees who are ready understand their brand and know how to drive their brand across key touchpoints and deliver a great branded experience. When all employees are aligned to their brand, a branded culture is created from top to bottom.

The reason why this is so powerful is due in part to the inherent approach on ensuring that your people are aligned to what your brand stands for. Throughout my career one of the best ways I have found for brands to produce results is to establish a brand driven culture focused on producing a brand that can make a difference in the lives of its employees. Not only is this critical for the success of your brand it is also the basis for the continual growth and the building of a world class brand that provides world class experiences both internally and externally.

Purpose

This mini e-book really serves a few purposes:
1. It is meant to stress the importance of internal branding in an organisation
2. It is meant to give you tips to build your brand from within
3. Lastly, it is meant to serve as an inspiration for you to take a personal stance on implementing and aligning your organisation's brand with the employees of your organisation

Remember if you want a great brand on the outside, start by looking from within. Employees are the most important assets a company can leverage on to transform itself in the market and establish a stronger brand connection with its customers.

THE STORY OF INTERNAL BRANDING

Strong internal brands reflect an organisation's culture by providing a brand promise that goes beyond the external brand image to shape the entire organisation. In a nutshell, Internal Branding is about aligning employee commitment to delivering the brand promise of the organisation.

Sartan and Schumann defined internal branding as: "how a business builds and packages its identity, from its origins and values, what it promises to deliver to emotionally connect employees so that they in turn deliver what a business promises to customer".

For internal branding to be successful, companies and organisations must begin with a strong brand strategy that drives the brand through operating principles in every area of the organisation.

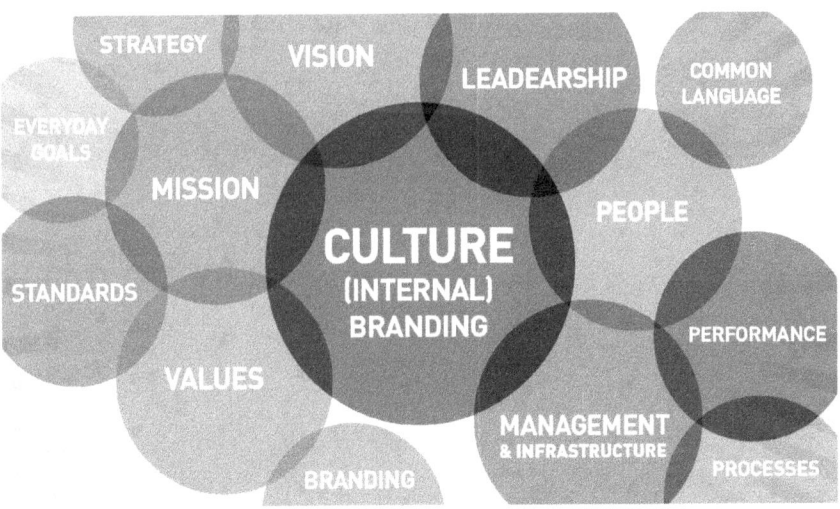

Our 10 principles will provide you with key ideas that you can use to build your internal brand and create a branded culture in your organisation.

The first step in the
acquisition of wisdom is
silence,
the second listening,
the third memory,
the fourth practice,
the fifth teaching others.

- Solomon Ibn Gabirol

PRINCIPLE 1

Give your Employees a Cause, not a Job

People want to contribute, not just to conform.

PRINCIPLE 1

Give them a Cause not a Job

Most internal branding programmes broadcast but they do not engage. They lay out rules and tell people what is going to happen, instead of presenting the case for why things need to change and how each person can be involved. People want to contribute, not just to conform. Strong internal branding programmes work because they arouse curiosity, pique interest and invite participation. Bad programmes simply tell people what is going to happen and when.

As Walt Disney said, 'You can dream, create and build the most wonderful place in the world, but it requires people to make the dream a reality'. Perhaps that is why Disney does not have staff. They have cast members, 120,000 of them worldwide. They come to work to create magic and their live the vision of the brand, which is "To make people happy"

The best branded culture changes work on two levels simultaneously: We and I. There's a big idea, a promise for everyone to believe in and to be stimulated by - and there's a personal driver. A company which we had consulted for had a strong blue element to their brand: BLUE stood for their brand values of Bold, Leading, Understanding and Exceeding Expectations, their logo was blue, their shops were blue themed, their collaterals were blue. To align employees to the brand, we helped them create a culture of Blue Blood, where everyone is blue-blooded because it is the sign-up credo that courses through the arteries of every person who works there. It gives every individual the driver they need - and it provides the collective lifeblood of belief that the company needs to compete successfully.

> **Quick Tip:**
>
> Develop an employee value proposition that is about your brand, what is stands for and what it promises to your employee. Make it about them and train your people to believe in it and make it their cause.

PRINCIPLE 2

Listen to your Employees

Measure. Measure. Measure

Listen to your Employees

PRINCIPLE 2

One of the most important factors that drives every employee to reach their goals is employee motivation. Your employees are your greatest assets and no matter how efficient your technology and equipment may be, it is meaningless if not for the effectiveness and efficiency of your staff. Listen to them and find out what makes them tick. Take your feedback from the customers and marry the two. Build your brand based on this information. Employees lose their motivation when they are not given importance. Make them feel that they are essential by listening to them. Employees are the lifeblood of your organisation and they are a rich source of information. Their opinions and feedback play an important role to the organisation's welfare. Listening to your employees helps them feel that they have an essential part of the business, and responsible for its success.

Listening to them can take many forms, such as meetings, personal phone calls, memos, group meetings, conferences or personal letters. Each employee's opinion needs to be heard and taken into consideration. Do not take them for granted or they will lose their interests to improve and contribute to the organisation's growth. Make them feel that they are important in your organisation.

When listening to them, look for areas of feedback specific to their understanding of the brand, their belief in the brand, advocacy, loyalty and engagement. Learn to spot gaps in what is lacking in employee understanding of the brand and solve it. Look for opportunities to leverage.

Quick Tip:

Here are some tools you can use to get feedback:

1. Roundtable discussions and Focus Groups
2. Employee Brand Perception Audits
3. Employee Satisfaction and Motivation survey
4. Observation
5. Reasons for leaving the company
6. Customer Feedback
7. Key employee touchpoint analysis
8. Grapevine

PRINCIPLE 3

Lead your Employees to the Level of Passionate Commitment

The true road to pre-eminent success in any line is to make yourself a master in that line.

PRINCIPLE 3

Lead your Employees to the Level of Passionate Commitment

Are your employees fully engaged? Employee commitment is what makes people say "I am proud of working here". Listening to your employee's needs is the key to employee commitment. Today, we need a new kind of leader, someone who not only creates goals and defines passion but also has the ability to make employees at every level of the organisation feel and share the same level of passion. Internal branding is more than just about organisational structure. Your employees can be thought of as "internal customers" giving their time, effort and commitment for the organisation in return of recognition, appreciation, respect and remuneration of course.

Ask your front-line workers, managers and support staff what you do as an organisation that is a real source of pride, what your key values are and in what ways are you improving people's lives. Hire the right people by taking personality tests for job applicants to determine whether they have the ingredients to contribute to your organisation's brand and what it stands for. Align those tests and interviews with your brand DNA. Organisations that can successfully harness employee commitment achieve strong delivery of their brand promise, which in turn leads to several distinct competitive advantages such as a workforce committed to your brand success.

> **Quick Tip:**
>
> Organise an employee brand day and fill the day with powerful stories about what it means to be committed to the brand. Get your leaders and champions to be part of this day. End the day by giving each employee a brand book which illustrates the power and belief of their brand.

PRINCIPLE 4

Create Brand Champions

Create champions that will help you fight for the cause of your brand.

Create Brand Champions

PRINCIPLE 4

Brand Champions are advocates who promote or refer your brand to others within and outside your organisation. They are passionate and committed to your brand. Your employees are the most critical part of your organisation, and these key internal assets are powerful resources that extend far beyond your marketing department. The key is to find those employees that are willing to act as advocates for your brand and if you cannot find them, create them.

Get your key employees to be raving fans of your own brand, get them to speak openly and honestly about your organisation's virtues, and encourage them to share their pride for their own and your organisation's work. Your employees can be your broadcasters, for example 'bloggers', 'facebookers', 'twitterers', etc. Know who your broadcasters are, allow them to be creative in improving their roles and job and reward them.

We knew of an employee, Thomas, who surfed the net and made it a point to defend or promote his company and their products entirely on his own. It was Thomas' passionate faith and respect for the brand of his company that made him willing to do whatever it would take to have that brand be a part of his lifestyle - performing as passionately and as hard as necessary to help his favourite brand continually perform at a higher level.

In the work that we do for organisations we create mini teams of champions across departments with the objective of activating and energising the brand from within. When you have a team of Brand Champions, they will fight for the cause for the brand at the frontlines, as well as act as catalysts to building your brand across the organisation. Another key project that we embarked on, was to help employees in an organisation revamp their business profiles on LinkedIn and get them to create branded content that positioned them as brand champions and at the same time drove brand awareness to their networks.

Quick Tip:

Get a team of Brand Champions together from various departments and get them to plan a series of activities and communication ideas to build the brand across the organisation.

PRINCIPLE 5

Deliver a Consistent Brand Message to your Employees

Internal branding emphasizes the overarching message that defines your brand culture and solidifies it.

PRINCIPLE 5

Deliver a Consistent Brand Message to your Employees

How consistently is your brand message communicated to every employee? Consistency is the key in any brand. There are times in our consultancy work where we have seen the collaterals of the brand preaching one message but yet the leaders are doing the exact opposite.

Internal branding emphasises the overarching message that defines your brand culture and solidifies your brand promise. Internal branding strategy must ensure that every interaction a customer has with your brand message must be uniform. The brand message is delivered consistently through each and every communication with your existing employees and potential candidates. Delivering a strong brand message to your employees leads to the delivery of a resonating brand message at every key touchpoint.

The first step is to identify all the key touchpoints in a brand. Next, create the brand message that can be most effectively used in that touchpoint. Next embed the brand message in voicemail messages, newsletters, annual reports, websites, and in one-on-one informal communications. Lastly, ensure that everyone understands and follows the brand, especially leaders of the organisation. Essentially, they have to walk the talk. Once every employee knows how to translate the brand message consistently, customers will be exposed to a well-tuned branding machine, drumming to the same beat.

Quick Tip:

List out your key touchpoints and measure the alignment of these touchpoints to your brand. Check if your employees are delivering these touchpoints consistently. Run touchpoint workshops to help them map their own personal customer touchpoint moments and teach them how to align your brand effectively in these workshops.

PRINCIPLE 6

Create Alignment Between a Compelling Employee Promise and Delivery

The face a company presents to its customers and the general public is largely a reflection of the face it presents to its employees

Create Alignment Between a Compelling Employee Promise and Delivery

PRINCIPLE 6

What is the promise you are making that really matters to your employees? Your employee brand promise should be consistent with your customer brand promise and your devotion to delivering on the promise should be complete. Strong internal brands reflect an organisation's culture by providing not only a customer brand promise but also a compelling employee promise that goes beyond the surface to shape the entire organisation.

Create an environment of respect and dignity among your employees. Only when the employee promise and the organisational structure have been aligned should organisations be looking at delivering the customer experience itself.

We worked with an organisation in Singapore that stressed that regardless of rank or file every employee had a role to play and would be treated with respect and equality. Through internal communication and training, we drove that message across the brand. One year after our campaign we were delighted when we saw a write-up in the papers about the organisation. When employees were interviewed by the media, they said that they were not just merely treated as employees, but they were treated like family. Regardless of their designation, they were treated with respect and dignity as promised by the brand. The employee promise that was made to them by the Brand was delivered! Treat your employees the way you would want to be treated and ensure that you treat them as well as you treat your customers.

> **Quick Tip:**
>
> Develop a compelling employee brand promise statement that is consistent with your customer brand promise. Ensure that it is communicated and reflected across key touchpoints. Finally, a promise should never be broken so ensure that everyone keeps to the employee and customer promises!

PRINCIPLE 7

Ensure your Employees Deliver a Branded Customer Experience

It is the emotional connection with employees on the inside so they in turn can connect with the people from the outside.

PRINCIPLE 7

Ensure your Employees Deliver a Branded Customer Experience

Touchpoints define the borderlines between the customer's worlds and yours. One of the reasons why organisations fail to deliver a branded customer experience is because employees are not provided with the tools and empowerment necessary to deliver extraordinary experiences across key touchpoints. There is no way to deliver great customer experience if employees cannot align themselves to these touchpoints or even deliver an inconsistent brand experience. But you cannot just "expect" employees to do what is right. You need to help your employees better serve customers with investments in training and enabling tools that will allow them to improve that experience. Ensure that they have knowledge of key touchpoints and how to align themselves to these touchpoints. Help them map out their entire customer's journey and help them fit your brand in that journey.

We worked with Samuel, managing director of a renowned software company, who had a problem with their sales. They had learned that 50 percent of their expected customers were not buying from them. We began our research to find out what was the problem. Our work included inviting customers for roundtable discussions. We also asked them about brand perception, touchpoint alignment, service quality and interaction with employees. Lastly, we also talked to employees to find out their take on this problem. We came to discover that the customers' problem was with their experience interacting with employees. Customers said that employees were not that knowledgeable and well-versed with the product. They also indicated that employees were more interested in selling rather than advising them. Interestingly the brand had promised their customers that they were a trusted advisor and they were all about customer relationships - something the brand was not keeping to according, to their customers. On probing deeper, we realised that employees were not engaged with the brand and lacked a sense of ownership for the brand to build these crucial relationships.

We worked with building ownership for the brand through developing an internal brand platform and an employee brand promise. We also built a customer touchpoint map and drove brand knowledge and belief by training employees on fulfilling the customer brand promise across the touchpoints. We also put into place an internal communications plan as well as a rewards and recognition program. The result was that customers started receiving a branded customer experience that resonated with the brand. Employees were now more engaged and empowered to deliver the brand promise.

Quick Tip:

Plot your customer touchpoints and create a branded experience at each touchpoint! Ensure that you get your people trained to deliver the experience.

PRINCIPLE 8

Build Brand Leaders

Leaders matter, but leadership matters more.

Build Brand Leaders

PRINCIPLE 08

"Leaders matter but leadership matters more." How many of you can say that we have experienced a dynamic and gifted leader who engaged all of us and drove us to great heights in our organisation. However, what happens when that leader moves on? You see Leadership matters more because it is linked not to a person but to the process of building leaders. However, leadership has got to stay true to the brand. If your brand is like a Virgin which is daring, fun-loving and passionate, then it is safe to say you need leaders in that mould. Leaders who are risk-takers, who possess a sense of humour and who are passionate about their brands and employees.

The actions of senior managers have a fundamental bearing on generating a culture that supports the brand. At Tesco, senior management talks about facilitating a culture that upholds the internal brand promise of 'treat each other the way you like to be treated'.

Many people mistake brand leaders in an organisation to be just the top level management but for us everyone is a leader.

Does your company have a culture where people from all functions are on a mission to build the brand, where they all see themselves as brand leaders or does it have a work environment where people just 'get the job done?'. What processes have you in place to ensure that you brand your leadership ie. Setting frameworks and processes to guide leaders to behave and perform in alignment to the brand.

> **Quick Tip:**
>
> Place the brand at the centre of what your company does and how your people work together. Get all your leaders to trace their decisions, behaviours and conversations with your employees back to their impact on the customer promise and the brand. Lastly, invest in leadership development solutions such as our Brand Leadership program to support managers so that they can effectuate personal leadership and brand culture changes that will unlock the potential of their people to meet the brand promise.

PRINCIPLE 9

Ensure that you Recruit On-Brand Employees

When you hire using your brand as a foundation, you get employees who believe in your brand.

PRINCIPLE 9

Ensure that you Recruit On-Brand Employees

You are recruiting the best employees for your organisation's needs. You want talented employees who fit your brand. Your recruitment strategies are critical in attracting these people. Brand strategy is crucial to the sustainable growth of all companies. However, some executives focus on building brands only for their products and make light of recruiting the right people for their brands.

I have seen global brands with the most amazing marketing brochures but with the most misaligned employer branding advertisements. Maybe it is because they think that a recruiting brand should be independent of their corporate brand. That is so wrong! In fact, the recruiting brand is a key element of the corporate brand since it communicates the organisation's values, goals and brand culture to talented candidates you want to attract. Ensure your employer branding advertisements communicate your brand clearly to attract the right people.

But on top of attracting the right people, ensure that during the interview process you ask questions related to your brand so that you ensure that there is a fit to your brand. When you hire, you will have to look at the people who fit in with your brand. If your brand is about fun then hiring someone who is not fun despite having the right skills might not be ideal to the fit for what your brand stands for. For a recent client we worked with, we created an On-Brand Recruitment program where we created a framework to select and evaluate the right candidates to the brand. Remember that the person can have all the talent in the world but if they are not aligned to the brand, then you will have an unhappy employee and a disappointed employer.

> **Quick Tip:**
>
> Create a Recruitment Checklist with your Brand Values listed. Write a description of the person you expect to hire based on these values. Train your hiring team to ask questions related to your brand.

PRINCIPLE 10

Recognize and Reward

Letting workers know they are appreciated is of year-round importance for employers.

Recognize and Reward

PRINCIPLE 10

Most organisations have some type of rewards program for their customers, and many have employee retention programs, but not that many have rewards and recognition programs for employees who demonstrate on-brand behaviour. If your organisation is going to get buy-in from employees for your brand and culture, then you will need to create programs that reward employees who demonstrate the behaviour you want.

This strategy will not only reward those who show the type of commitment to your brand that you want, but the rewards and recognition program will help all employees get it! Do not just assume everyone understands your brand strategy and will always be on-brand. This recognition is valuable to not only reward those brand champions who live your brand, but help others understand what you expect and how to embrace your brand strategy.

Other ways of recognizing employee brand champions can include highlighting employees on your websites, in your newsletters, annual reports and other communications tools. Of course, the obvious is rewarding on-brand behaviour at annual performance evaluation and salary increment time.

One client we worked with implemented a month-long reward and recognition program call "Brand Heroes". Employees who performed on-brand, had incentives such as a day off and shopping vouchers. They were also interviewed for the monthly newsletter and were featured on their wall of fame. At the end of the year, the best of the best were invited to share the secret of their success at staff conferences ensuring that they were also championing the brand from within.

> **Quick Tip:**
>
> Link your Rewards and Recognition program with your Brand. Recognize delivery of brand values, On-Brand behaviours and communication as well as Brand Championing. Create a rewards system based on execution of the above and you will be on your way to creating a strong internal brand.

BONUS PRINCIPLE

Symbols, Stories and Rituals

Creating a culture requires a set of tools to drive your brand from within.

BONUS PRINCIPLE

Symbols, Stories and Rituals

When it comes to creating branded cultures, it is often the use of rituals, symbols and stories that drives brand connection and culture from within. Let us dive right in.

Symbols are objects, acts, qualities or events that convey meaning to others. Within an organisation, one can use symbols to drive meaning for the brand. For example, in one organisation whose brand was predominantly Red and whose values were to protect/care for the environment, the brand team created Red Day. On this symbolic day, the company closed its operations and sent all its employees to clean beaches and parks and also raised funds for the environment. This was a powerful symbolic event for this organisation not just to their employees but also to their customers who sometimes even joined in.

Stories are narratives based on events in your organisation. Stories could be about your brand values, brand champions, history and so on. Storytelling is a very powerful brand-building technique. Telling your unique brand story can go a long way toward determining your brand's success. Great stories give big voices to your culture and what you stand for. For one of our clients, we created a brand storybook of employee stories which featured employees across the brand and their experiences about how they made a difference for the brand. It was extremely well-received with several sequels because of its strong personal touch.

Rituals are the activities and ceremonies, planned and unplanned, that celebrate important occasions and accomplishments in the organisation. One of my all-time favourite rituals is that of the Ritz-Carlton Line-Up. Every day around the world, employees of Ritz-Carlton make time for their "line-up" meeting before they start work. The purpose of the line-up is to align themselves to their brand principles and share success stories and application of their brand across their touchpoints.

> **Quick Tip:**
>
> In today's world, it is extremely critical to drive your brand from within. Start with your brand values and create symbols, stories and rituals around them. Then start to communicate this to your employees across your key touchpoints.

CONCLUSION

Let's Begin!

If you do not have a clarity of purpose to what your brand stands for, now is the time to make that happen. If your people are not pulling together in complete brand harmony now is the time to make it happen. It is about time that organisations start to recognise that their most important marketing assets are their employees and their interpretation of their brand.

1. Be Clear why you want to change or impact by doing your internal brand research
2. Build your Brand Champion team to plan this change and act as a catalyst for your brand
3. Make sure the leaders get involved and ensure they are committed to brand engagement throughout the company
4. Get your employees involved and empowered
5. Train your Employees to Live the Brand through the right behaviours and brand-driven mindset
6. Make the delivery of your brand across every touchpoint aligned and consistent to what the brand stands for
7. Work with an experienced brand consultant so that you do not end up being self-indulgent

> "Internal Branding is about aligning employees' commitment to deliver the brand promise of the organisation."

How Can We Help?

OUR INTERNAL BRAND FRAMEWORK

So you want to build your internal brand? As an internal branding consultancy, we have been approached by numerous corporate clients across diverse industries attempting to align their employees to their brand. Organisations are starting to realize the Power of building a brand from within and using their employees as a key marketing asset.

Who should own the project?

The answer is that HR and Corporate Communications need to own this project together with Sales, Operations and Marketing. It is a combined effort and of course it cannot happen without the buy-in from the top. Let us share with you our 4-Step Approach to Internal Branding Alignment.

The 4-Step Approach consists of

1. Employee Research
Optimise employee engagement through research

- Communication Audit
- Employee Diaries
- Brand Inside Research Tool™
- Employee Brand Scorecard
- Brand Metrics

2. Internal Branding Strategy
Develop a global internal strategy to grow your brand

- Employee Value Proposition
- Employee Behaviour Map
- Employee Values Map
- Employee Brand Development
- Employer Brand Platform

3. Employee Training
Drive employee engagement through trainings and workshops

- Brand Strategy Workshop
- Brand Champion Workshop
- Live the Brand Workshop
- Brand Leadership Workshop
- Branded Customer Experience Workshop

4. Brand Reinforcement
Reinforce your brand with every communication

- Internal/Employee Communications
- Employee Guidelines
- Strategic HR Integration
- Employee Reward, Recognition & Retention Programme
- Internal & External Measurement

OUR KEYNOTES AND WORKSHOPS

- **Experience Branding: Establish Deep Audience Connection Through Our Brand Experience Framework**
  Learn how to utilise consumer insights and our proprietary brand experience framework to create a deep and lasting connection between your brand and your audiences.

- **Lessons From The Legends: Asia Or Global**
  In this powerful program, deep dive into the strategies, challenges and ideas from some of the most successful brands in Asia/World to apply in your own businesses to help you grow and stand out.

- **Ultimate Brand Strategy: Powerful Strategies To Stand Out / Brand Blueprint: Creating A Powerful Brand Framework For Success**
  Create a winning Brand through a strategic blueprint so that your brand stands out from the competition.

- **Branding 5.0: New Media, New Conversations, New Experiences**
  In the age of Disruption, what are the cutting-edge ideas that can help you engage your customers better and deliver a branded experience.

- **Sell The Brand: Using The Power Of Brand To Drive Sales**
  Transform your approach to sales and drive brand value for long-term brand success.

- **Internal Branding: Growing Your Brand From Within / The Brand Champion Mindset**
  This program focuses on helping organisations create Brand champions and how organisations can instill a branded culture that is aligned to their brand and people.

- **TURN Me ON: Strategies To Build Your Personal Brand**
  Learn how to stand out, make a difference, be memorable and deliver a worldclass brand through our proprietary 5D framework of Personal Branding strategies.

- **Once Upon A Brand: The Power Of Brand Story Telling**
  This program covers the importance of crafting a Brand story that is compelling and authentic as well as leveraging the power of personal connection through stories to create lasting relationships with your customers.

- **Branded Customer Experience: Staging ExtraOrdinary Branded Experiences**
  Create a brand driven Customer Experience (CX) that turns your customers into raving fans.

- **Brand Leadership: Leading from Within**
  Leaders need to be driven by Brand. Learn how leaders can create brand champions and a branded culture that is driven by what their brand stands for.

TALK TO US

Jerome Joseph
CSP, Global Speaking Fellow, PMC, Chief Experience Officer
M +65 9271 6973
E jerome@jeromejoseph.com

> The practice of internal brand must obtain a permanent status in every organisation.

www.ingramcontent.com/pod-product-compliance
Lightning Source LLC
Chambersburg PA
CBHW071441220526
45469CB00004B/1616